Inspired, Informed & Infused

Linda S. Oviatt

DEDICATION

No one goes through this life alone. We are assisted from the moment we take our first breath to our dying breath. Every stage of life brings people across our path. Some bring joy, some teach, some test, some love, and some pass through for a brief moment with a smile on a cloudy day. There are many.

The women God has brought into my life to support and encourage me to push through and write this book are precious. I dedicate this book to them. They have helped me find my voice. I have been encouraged to do everything from standing on a chair and declaring what I believe, to crying through an emotional release. I have been given sanctuary and anointed with oils. There have been endless phone calls and words of encouragement. They have read, dissected, and given honest feedback throughout the process.

I am truly blessed. Thank you.

CONTENTS

AWAKENING

Eze. 47:12 *Along the banks of the river, on this side and that, will grow all kinds of trees used for food; their leaves will not wither, and their fruit will not fail. They will bear fruit every month, because their water flows from the sanctuary. Their fruit will be for food, and their leaves for* **medicine**.

On one notable occasion, a doctor said something that particularly galvanized me into my journey to health. I was sitting in an exam room, feeling pretty vulnerable, in an ugly gown with nothing underneath, when the doctor walked in. He looked at me, he looked at the chart, he looked at me again, he looked at the chart once more, and then he asked what was going on. After my lengthy and detailed reply, he just looked at me. His glorious reply was, "You're just aging on schedule."

There are not too many men out there who are going to survive telling a hormonal woman they're aging on schedule. It was a dangerous gamble!

The doctor said that he wanted to simply increase the medication that I was on so that I would stay comfortable. He said, "As you age, your symptoms are going to get worse. We'll just increase the medication and you'll be fine." And I sat there thinking, "Dude, I am not going to be continually increasing my medication. There has got to be a better way. And who's flipping schedule am I on? I haven't seen this calendar. Do you know on which day I'm supposed to develop arthritis? Listen, buddy, I've got plans. I have a daughter. I haven't even seen her graduate from high school. She hasn't had a wedding. I haven't had a grandchild. I'm not going to do this in a wheelchair while supporting your Ferrari payments with my medical bills! Sorry, that's not happening."

I believe that YOU can set the schedule. The power of wellness is in your hands! Today, I help people live intentional lives to know truth and to live wide awake in a time that most of our country is asleep to the dangers around us. And I am thriving....not dying.

Many people tend to compartmentalize who they are, taking on certain roles, scheduling activities carefully, and living life by labels either self assigned or ascribed to us by someone else. Some of those labels regarding our health seem to both define and limit us. It is easy to lose sight of who we are meant to be when the labels we wear seem to put us in rigid boxes. However, we are all God's creation, and He gave us a whole plan. We don't have to accept the labels given to us, we can exist in the glory of His perfect plan for us.

It's like I had hats on a wall, and I had to just switch hats for each individual role. Instead, I can take off all those hats and proclaim, "I am a child of the King. I am protected. I have all the knowledge I need. I just need to use the mind that He gave me, think that new thought, make those connections, do the research, and He will help me get that wisdom."

James 1:5
"If any of you lacks wisdom, you should ask God, who gives generously to all without finding fault, and it will be given to you."

Focusing on your health can feel overwhelming, but it's not impossible. I wasn't born a diseased person and the choices I made had consequences. I didn't know what I didn't know, but they were uninformed choices and consequences. Now, I can make informed choices to change those consequences. I can reverse a lot of it. Once I began learning how to take charge of my own health, my path unfolded before me and I haven't looked back.

I'm writing this book to share the holisticness of taking care of yourself, not only for longevity and health, but also for God's glory. It's a beautiful marriage of knowledge because it was there to begin with. Somehow, health and God get separated when we create Wednesday night Bible studies, where we learn how to be kind and gentle to others, and yet we never approach what God gave us for our health and taking care of our bodies.

My journey to health began back when I had a hysterectomy and was thrown into instant menopause, which was a boatload of pandemonium. I had cold hands and cold feet. I had mind fog. I couldn't stay awake. I couldn't manage my weight. It took me back to being a kid in junior high school when my nickname was "the whale". I had fought my weight for such a long time and my mental state was continuing to decline, along with my health.

I had tried everything. I had gone through every diet. Every time I went to the grocery store, I was inundated with twenty or so magazines that gave the diet of the month and the thing that you're doing wrong and the vitamin that you need to take. I went through hundreds of dollars and none of it worked.

One day, I received an email from somebody that lived in my old neighborhood. It was a random email and I didn't even know her, but she was giving an essential oil class. I was intrigued, so I wrote her back and said, "I think my name is still on an old mailing list, but I'm curious, may I still come and see?" She said yes, and I went and listened and was fascinated. I took the information and went home with it, thought about it, and then spent some time researching. It was a bit overwhelming, but at the same time it wasn't much of an investment compared to all that I had already done. I had nothing to lose and everything to gain.

So, I got the kit, started going to the classes, and eagerly jumped in! I did exactly what she said and in six weeks, I had my mind back. My energy level had increased. I was slowly, but surely, making these changes while learning about diet, nutrition, and supplements. I started learning what I needed and also learning what I didn't need.

I was fascinated by the information. A whole new world opened up for me. I learned about toxins. I learned about bioaccumulation and about its effects on the body. I learned how to *reverse* the damage. To find out more on how compounds and constituents in food, plants, and medicine react in the body, I became a "Certified Aromatherapist"

The biggest change came in the form of getting hazardous chemicals out of the house. It was a huge piece of the puzzle! I couldn't believe the change! I haven't struggled with weight since I began this journey. I'm not telling you that you can use lemon oil to drain your lymph system every day and eat a Twinkie. That isn't going to happen! I can, however, tell you that I'm now able to make better decisions using all the tools that are at my disposal and make truly informed choices.

At first, my faith wasn't a part of my health journey. As I started diving into this whole oily world, I began reading books and seeing how God's plan with plants and nature was so precise and beautiful. God was the first aromatherapist! He made man and He put him in a garden! I started making these connections and realizing that He gave us dominion over plants. He gave us the trees and the leaves for healing. I started understanding things in a different way.

This book is designed to be an inspiration to help YOU make changes. It will inform you about why these changes are important and give you a few infused ideas to start the journey. God does have a plan for you and yes, there are essential oils in the Bible! Just ask the Magi! They brought the Christ child two of the most valuable things on the planet - Frankincense and Myrrh! The gifts provided for his health and financial well being, and I assure you, Mary loved that Myrrh. Let's find out why.

Each chapter will focus on a different body system. I will INSPIRE you with God's Word, INFORM you on the function of each body system and then help you

INFUSE your life with essential oil suggestions to support that system. You will never read the Christmas story or the Bible with the same eyes again!

2 Timothy 3:16-17
16 All Scripture is God-breathed and is useful for teaching, rebuking, correcting and training in righteousness, 17 so that the servant of God may be thoroughly equipped for every good work.

 **INSPIRED**

I am a believer in the Word of God, and I was thoroughly entrenched in the Western medicine approach to wellness and treatment of the body and emotions. Perhaps like you, I was deeply skeptical about Eastern medicine beliefs and practices. So much so, that I thought essential oils and herbs were either not Christian or old school or even worse, unholy.

I didn't realize that I could find health advice in the Bible. We all jump to the so-called 'greater lessons' of love, money, serving, and forgiveness, and we totally miss the health lessons in the Word of God. Those little nuances that were deemed worthy enough to be included in the Word. Why? If it was useless information and not meant to be carried down from generation to generation, it wouldn't have been included. I learned to stop associating God's natural gifts with mysticism and began to see the power in His creation, His provision, and the graciousness of a loving and creative God.

Scripture I had read before began to take on new meaning. I had to let go of my skepticism and disbelief and embrace the fact that there was more to learn. I previously had total faith in the traditional Western medicine approach, but now I had questions. And I wanted answers. As I dove into the world of essential oils and food as medicine, I saw things differently. It might have had a lot to do with the fact that my mind fog was finally lifted. Literally, I began using essential oils and supplements that my body could actually use and foods that would heal. I could actually think again!

I saw the passage in Exodus on oils. I read with wonder about Ester and her use of Myrrh and was amazed when I learned about the Frankincense and Myrrh given by the Kings to the newborn King. Jesus was anointed by a woman with expensive nard, an anointing oil.

There are hundreds of references to oils in the Bible! They were in common use and simply a part of everyday knowledge.

God has provided us with so much!!!

The word *"inspiration"*, translated from Greek, means "God-breathed". In classic Roman times, *inspirare* meant "to breathe deeply" and figuratively speaking "to instill [something] in the heart or in the mind of someone".

This section of the book is where I want to inspire you. To instill a new thought into your mind. To get to your heart. To encourage you to take a deep breath and let go. Just breathe out.

I do not know where you are in your life as you read the words on this page. You picked up this book for a reason. Perhaps you, too, are looking for answers as I was.

I want to INSPIRE you on your search!

Plants of the Bible

There are thousands of references to plants in the Bible. The following are a handful that we get essential oils from:

Bay Ps 37:35
Calamus   Exodus 30:23   mentioned 5 times
Cassia Ps 45:8 mentioned 3 times
Cedar Lev 14:49 mentioned 73 times
Cinnamon   Ex 30:23 mentioned 4 times
Coriander Numbers 11:7 mentioned 2 times
Cypress Isaiah 41:19 mentioned 22 times
Dill   Matt 23:23 mentioned 3 times
Frankincense   Matt 2:11 mentioned 23 times
Galbanum   Ex 30:34
Hyssop Psalm 51:7 mentioned 12 times
Juniper 1Kings 19:4 mentioned 4 times
Mint Matt 23:23 mentioned 2 times
Myrrh Esther 2:12 mentioned 16 times
Myrtle Nehemiah 8:15 mentioned 6 times
Onycha Exodus 30:34
Rose of Sharon Song of Solomon 2:1
Sandalwood 1Kings 10:11 mentioned 6 times
Spikenard John 12:3 mentioned 5 times

(For in-depth, yet easy to understand, information on Biblical oils, please consider the book <u>Oils of the Bible</u> by Joshua Graff, MAR. It is considered to be a must-have book for your health and wellness toolbox. He brings history to life with stories of the use of the plants in ceremonies, building, health, and so much more. This list came from his book.)

I bridged the gap between allopathic (the practice of traditional or Western medical care of the body) with alternative or complementary care with the use of essential oils by simply reading the Bible with new eyes!

We like to read the Bible and piecemeal it to tailor it to our lives. We agree with some statements, but think not everything really applies to us now. I call this the Christian buffet style of living. We are leaving some condiments on the buffet and like salt, it makes you thirsty for more. I wanted to know more!

My goals have moved from surviving to thriving. Instead of a goal of not being on as many medications to manage my disease, I now have a goal to write books to help others. I used to have a homeless ministry where I served hundreds. Today, my goal is to inspire audiences of thousands to live out the purpose He assigned for them in abundant wellness.

1 Peter 4:10 commands us, *"Each of you should use whatever gift you have received to serve others, as faithful stewards of God's grace in its various forms."*

I am 65 years old, and I have not taken a single steroid, antibiotic, or over the counter stomach medication since 2014. I am thriving and growing younger every year. My father, at this age, was already on several medications.

By the time he passed away just weeks after his 80th birthday, there must have been 30 bottles of medicine on the kitchen table. My mother had lost her mind to Alzheimer's and passed away earlier. My father's final words to me were to go and live life, explore new things, and experience the world before I was too old and just giving my money to doctors. That's far from a picture of hope or anything to look forward to. That's not thriving or living abundantly.

I am living abundantly and want you to live well in abundance too.

Eph 2:10 says, *"You are God's masterpiece! He has created us anew in Christ to do the good things He planned for us!"*

1Cor 6:20 says *"You were bought with a price. So glorify God in your body".*

In the body of Christ, I am a mouth. I have not always used this 'gift' properly, however, through God's grace, we are all a work in progress. I have learned the hard way to basically be quiet and listen. I learned to be teachable, moldable, and to allow myself to be used by God to further His kingdom. He has much for us to do, and we are of no service when we are sick and tired.

He is using the gifts He gave me. I love to share what I have learned. My head is no longer stuck in the sand. My eyes are wide open.

God is most interested in what He can do through us. All healing is delivered by God.

Keep your body strong so you can serve others!
Honor it so you can accomplish God's mission for you!
Open your eyes to the provision he gave us in the
garden
to take care of your body for service.

INFORMED

The cost of healthcare in the United States was nearly
$10,000 per person, per year, as of 2017. (3) There's a
really nice, big word called "iatrogenic", and it is
defined as relating to illness caused by medical
examination, treatment, or a medical professional. It is
the third leading cause of death in the United States. I
don't want to be on that list, so my plan is to stay out of
the hospital as much as possible!

Because of the way God made me, this curious
questioner, I needed the science to back up what I was
learning. When I started putting modern science
together with the oils that they were using back in
Biblical times, I started realizing that God had a plan!
But humans, trusting their own wisdom, found ways to
make food and medicine faster and cheaper. However,
this has been to the detriment of our health.

What Was Before Medicine?

Did you know that essential oils may be the oldest and
some of the most powerful wellness promoting agents
known? Here's a timeline that beautifully illustrates how

essential oils have featured prominently at some pivotal points in time:

Third Day of Creation
Essential oils were given to us on the third day of creation for our well being. Well, technically, God created vegetation. He does give man dominion over the earth later in Genesis. Perhaps we should study why and how he provided for us.

7000 BC to 4000 BC
Anthropologists find evidence of fragrant plants being combined with fatty oils of olive and sesame to create Neolithic ointments.

3000 - 2000 BC
Egyptian records indicate that they were importing large quantities of myrrh.

1333 - 1323 BC
King Tutankhamen ruled Egypt and when his tomb was discovered in November 1922, they found some 50 alabaster (calcite) jars designed to hold 350 liters of oil. They were still as good as the day they placed them into his tomb.

100 BC
Rome reportedly consumed 2,800 tons of imported frankincense and 500 tons of myrrh per year.

50 BC
1st century AD Roman historian, Pliny, author of the 1st century AD Natural History, mentions 32 recipes prepared from rose oil, 21 from lily, 17 from violet, and 25 from pennyroyal.

The New Testament is filled with hundreds of references to oil, including frankincense and myrrh, brought to the Christ child.

1400 AD

During this time of the great plague, known as the Black Death, the king learned that robbers were stripping the dead of their jewelry and belongings. The robbers were perfumers and spice traders by profession and used essential oils of clove, cinnamon, lemon, eucalyptus, and rosemary rubbed all over their bodies and put oils in their masks for breathing.

1817

The 870-foot-long Ebers Papyrus was discovered. Dating back to 1500 BC it mentioned over 800 herbs and oils.

3 Doctors

1910-1940

In July 1910, Dr. Rene Maurice Gattefosse, a French chemist and perfumer, rediscovered the therapeutic value of essential oils in his family's perfumery business laboratory when he burned his arm quite severely. That accident began Gattefosse's extensive research of essential oils. He discovered their ability to penetrate the skin and enter into the body's internal organs and nervous system. He classified the way they affected the digestive system, our metabolism, nervous system and endocrine glands. He published a book, "Gattefosse's Aromatherapy", that contained his early findings for using essential oils for a very wide range of physical ailments. He coined the term *Aromatherapy*.

1940-1970

Dr. Jean Valnet (MD), a French scientist and army physician and surgeon, used tea tree essential oil to treat wounded soldiers during World War II when antibiotics ran out. His work established the development of the modern use of essential oils as a supplement to healthcare stemming from the success he had on the battlefield.

Late 1950s

Marguerite Maury began studying essential oils and how they could be used to penetrate the skin during a massage, a technique still practiced today. She also founded the practice of "individually prescribed" combinations of essential oils to suit the needs of the person being massaged.

20th Century

The US is 5% of the World's population.
We consume 75% of all the pharmaceuticals.
There are consequences to pharmaceutical called side effects. There is a lot of money in having people on medicines for life.

1973

In his book, "The Practice of Aromatherapy: A Classic Compendium of Plant Medicines and Their Healing Properties", Jean Valnet, MD writes, "Dr. Taylor of the University of Austin, Texas has observed that essential oils present more new compounds than the chemists of the whole world could analyze in a thousand years. We now know that they are mixtures of many powerful chemical constituents."

Because of their unique chemical structure, essential oils are able to penetrate the cell membrane of human cells, just as they do the cells of plants, carrying vital nutrients inside. Once inside the cell, "essential oils promote natural healing by stimulating and reinforcing the body's own mechanisms," says author Christine Wildwood in her book, "Holistic Aromatherapy".

It Begins with a Choice

This 'It' list came from a fellow oiler, Jodie Meschuk, and lists what 'it' can do.

The problems are all mine.
It could cause cancer. I stopped buying it.
It contributes to infertility. I couldn't have children.
It causes emotional problems. Like I need more??
It brings on digestive issues and weight problems.
Check! Check!
It makes your brain foggy. I couldn't think straight anymore.
It lowers your energy. I would fall asleep standing up!
It gives you bad skin. The list is too long...
It makes you sick with a terrible immune system.

'It' is in:
CANDLES. ROOM SPRAYS. PERFUMES. SKIN CARE. MAKEUP. LOTIONS. SHAMPOO. SOAPS. CLEANING PRODUCTS. FOOD. DRINKS.

'It' is harmful, damaging, and unnecessary chemicals like formaldehyde, fragrances, preservatives, dyes, parabens, phthalates, talc, sulfates, pesticides, herbicides, and about a million others that we are CHOOSING to expose ourselves to in the products we willingly buy. A lot of these ingredients that the US allows, many other countries around the world have actually banned.

I chose to stop buying products with chemicals that could harm me. I stopped buying foods that were packaged and so full of chemicals that they wouldn't even break down in landfills. I stopped buying meat full of antibiotics and hormones.

God gave you a body. You don't get a new one until you get to Heaven. Being a good steward of how you care for your earthly body is important.

Deu 30:19 *I call heaven and earth to record this day against you, that I have set before you life and death, blessing and cursing: therefore choose life, that both thou and thy seed may live.*

We have the power to change what we do, eat, buy, and use on our bodies from this day forward. We can approach the changes we want to make in a faith-filled way, and we can watch God work all things out for our good.

Romans 8:28 *And we know that in all things God works for the good of those who love him, who have been called according to his purpose.*

When I changed my system of thinking, I began to believe that I could change that schedule of dying given to me by the Western world. I had the power of wellness in my own hands, which God had given to me from the beginning of time!

Current health statistics paint a grim picture:

- In 2017, there were 884,700,000 (MILLION) doctor visits in the U.S.
    - Patients aged 45 years and up visit more in 2019 than 10 years ago.
    - 37% of visits were for chronic conditions
    - Average time spent with the patient…19 minutes
- 70% of the U.S. is on prescription drugs.
- 4,468,929,929 (BILLION) prescriptions were filled by Americans in 2016. That is an average of nearly *20* prescriptions PER PERSON.
- 78,964,222 (MILLION) Americans are on psychiatric drugs (ADHD, antidepressants, anti-anxiety, antipsychotic, etc.)
- 8,389,034 (MILLION) of those are our KIDS, including children UNDER 2 years old.
- NEONATAL & INFANT deaths are higher in the U.S. than other developed nations putting us on par with countries like Serbia & Malaysia.
- The U.S. has the HIGHEST rate of MATERNAL deaths of all developed countries in the world.
- There were over 230 industrial chemicals found in the umbilical cords of newborn babies.
- ONE THIRD of all babies born surgically in the U.S. are by Cesarean section.

- 70% of the U.S. is overweight with 30% being obese.
- The cost of "health care" in the U.S. is nearly $10,000 PER PERSON, PER YEAR (as of 2017). That is a life-time cost of over $750,000 PER PERSON.
- Iatrogenic (medical-caused) death is the THIRD leading cause of death in the U.S.

If you don't want to be one of the people on that list (or if you want to get OFF that list), it's time to take your health into your own hands!

The article cited in Consumer Reports from US Government data, lists 12 conditions for which people can attempt lifestyle changes before taking prescription medications: ADHD, back and joint pain, dementia, mild depression, heartburn, insomnia, low testosterone, osteopenia (bone loss), overactive bladder, prediabetes, prehypertension, and obesity.

YOU can change those statistics!
One step at a time. Day by day.

I believe you can thrive. In fact, I know you can! I have seen miraculous health improvements when people wake up and accept the fact they are the gatekeepers to their homes, their bodies, and their minds.

Start with one closet. One space. It can be a kitchen, bath, or laundry room to remove toxins. Start with one meal, one shelf in the refrigerator, or clean out a shelf of packaged foods. Learn to read labels. Open your mind to the use of essential oils instead of the pharmacy for immune boosting, sleep inducing, mood elevating, pain relieving, and even beautifying skin options.

INFUSED

It all started in a garden…

God spoke herbs and essential oils into existence at Creation when He formed the plants, trees, flowers, and shrubs and gave them to man (Genesis 1:29). They are gifts given for our service (Psalm 104:14; Ezekiel 47:12). Good gifts.

"The compounds comprising plant oils were spoken into existence when God created plants. These compounds are imbued with God's Word and God's intelligence, which is not measured in a laboratory, nor by any physical instrument…Synthetic compounds may be copies of the formulas of compounds found in essential oils, but they are lacking the subtle energies contained in natural substances." – David Steward, PhD, DNM, IASP

Let's get you on your journey,
through the garden and
look into taking care of your needs.

What is an Essential Oil?

Essential oils are aromatic and volatile liquids that come from the rind, bark, leaf, flower, or root of plants. It is the lifeblood and protection of the plant. These liquids are necessary for the life of the plant, the power to sustain their own life. A plant doesn't exactly bleed, but when you cut a plant, you see something like sap that assists the plant in healing itself. We never stop to think about it, but plants are pretty smart. This life blood is chemically complex and contains hundreds of compounds or constituents. It aids the plant in controlling infection, temperature, hormonal effects, wound healing, and attracting or repelling insects, birds, and animals. Extracting essential oils from plants is done with a process called distillation, most commonly by steam or water. The outcome is a highly concentrated essential oil, which will have the characteristic fragrance and properties of the plant from which it was extracted, including the plant's healing properties.

Plants store essential oils either in external secretory structures, which are found on the surface of the plant, like Basil, Lavender, Peppermint, or internal secretory structures, which are found inside the plant material, like Cinnamon, Citronella, and Bay Laurel. Sometimes we get three different oils from one plant! Consider the orange tree. We get Orange oil from the rind, Pettigrain is from the twigs and leaves, and Neroli is extracted from the blossoms.

The essential oils that protect the plants also protect us. The compounds and constituents that are adapting in plants, adapt in us. That's why you hear the term *adaptogenic* when people refer to essential oils. Synthetic drugs that are made by isolating one or two constituents are no match for bacteria or viruses which can easily adapt and mutate, making those drugs useless. Have you ever been told you have a Superbug and that there is nothing they can treat it with? Well, there are simply too many constituents within an essential oil for a virus to adapt to.

Some people refer to essential oils as alternative medicine. I prefer the term *complementary*. Aromatherapy simply offers you choices that have a therapeutic value that can be effective if used sensibly. All of the major physical systems of the body respond to aromatherapy in a positive manner.

Essential oils need to be used with good sense. Conventional medicine has its place and should certainly be included in health decisions, especially when it will provide the best results. The truth regarding the beneficial properties of essential oils has long been neglected and misunderstood by most in Western society. Today, we are the only culture not incorporating heavy spices, herbs, and oils into our daily regimen of nutrition. Essential oils are not wonder drugs. The oils are not here to treat, but to support our body. Your health isn't luck. It's good decisions.

What is Aromatherapy?

The Merriam-Webster Dictionary defines *aromatherapy* as "the inhalation or bodily application (as by massage) of fragrant essential oils (as from flowers and fruits) for therapeutic purposes."

"Aromatherapy is a natural, non-invasive modality designed to affect the whole person, not just the symptom or disease and to assist the body's natural ability to balance, regulate, heal and maintain itself by the correct use of essential oils." -- Jade Shutes

"The term 'aromatherapy' is misleading. In actuality, the oils exert much of their therapeutic effect through their pharmacological properties and their small molecular size, making them one of the few therapeutic agents to easily penetrate bodily tissues". - Kurt Schnaubelt, PhD: "Alternative Medicine: The Definitive Guide".

How to Use Essential Oils

There are basically three ways you can use essential oils to promote health and healing: ingestion, diffusion, and topical use. There are different models of use, a French, German and English model. The English model believes essential oils must be heavily diluted and discourages internal use. The Germans pretty much only inhale them. The French model includes topical application, inhalation, and taking them internally. The French methods are ONLY used when using the highest grade of THERAPEUTIC essential oils.

If you are only using an oil for the aroma or for soap making, then you can use oils from health food stores and through cheaper outlets online. If you want the therapeutic value of the oils, only use high quality oils. Cheap oils will yield no results and may make a situation worse. 100% pure Therapeutic Grade Essential oils, when used properly, are designed to enable the body to heal itself, not kill it or contribute to additional sickness or cause side effects.

INGESTING OILS

I follow the French model of aromatherapy, which says you can put them on the body, you can diffuse them, and you can internally take them. My argument to people that say, "Well you can't take them internally" is, "Do you eat pizza? Have you had lemonade?" Take a look at the food manufacturers! Coca-Cola is one of the largest food manufacturers that imports essential oils because there is lime and lemon oils in the ingredients. There's peppermint oil in your candy and mints. Have you gone and bought your bone broth lately? There is Rosemary in there. Is there a reason Rosemary is in there? Yes! Rosemary is a preservative, and that's why it is in your natural bone broth that you see on the shelves. Basically, you're ingesting them, no matter what you think.

I use oils in salad dressings, marinades, and I even make peppermint brownies! I teach a whole class on mocktails and cocktails. There are a lot of options and recipes out there!

DIFFUSION

If you have a pure therapeutic, botanical essential oil, you can open the bottle and the oil will diffuse. The molecules are very, very fine. Oils are a volatile liquid, which means that the molecules are very fast moving, and they disperse into the air very quickly. You open a bottle of peppermint, I guarantee you somebody's going to walk in the room and say, "I smell peppermint." You open a bottle of olive oil, nobody's going to say they smell olive oil, because it's a fatty oil and fat sticks together. You can diffuse oil with any natural fiber, for example cotton or wood. Do not use any synthetics because the oils may break down petrochemicals, so you don't want to use anything unnatural.

I have a diffuser in every room in the house!

TOPICALLY

You can also put oils on your body topically. There are a lot of oils that you can put directly on the body. Some of them need to be diluted with a carrier oil. Carrier oils are not essential, and there are many, such as coconut, olive, or grapeseed. How much you dilute them depends on the type of oil and whether you're using it on an infant, an elderly person, or a healthy person. They can be used in everything from shampoos to cream rinses, bath salts, body lotions, and toothpaste.

CHAPTER 1

THE CARDIOVASCULAR SYSTEM: THE HEART OF THE MATTER

 **INSPIRED**

Are you looking to push up daisies or are you embracing your vitality? Your heart is the most crucial organ in your body!

Our hearts are our life force. The word *heart* is mentioned around 500 times in the Bible, depending on which translation you study. God calls us to protect this vital organ in

Proverbs 4:23 *Above all else, guard your heart, for everything you do flows from it.*

According to the Bible, the heart is our spiritual center. Beyond its physical function of moving blood to all of our organs, it is the epicenter of our emotions and our desires. Jeremiah 17:10 says, *I the Lord search the heart and examine the mind, to reward each person according to their conduct, according to what their deeds deserve.* The importance of the heart shows up time and time again in the Bible as the gateway to our spiritual discernment and knowledge. The heart symbolizes love and loyalty and is a repository of peacefulness, generosity, and strength of character.

Psalms 57:7 *My heart is fixed, I will sing and give praise*

Acts 14:7 *fruitful seasons filling our hearts with food and gladness*

Mark 12:30 *And you shall* **love** *the Lord your God from your whole* **heart**

 **INFORMED**

The shape and beat of your heart can be used to verify your identity. God made each of us unique. He knows us intimately. To know the Lord, we must use the heart He gave us. In order to love Him with our whole hearts, we must take care of them. We need to care for not only our spiritual heart, but also our physical heart.

Currently, over 600,000 people in the United States die of heart disease every year -- that is approximately 1 in every 4 deaths. Heart disease is the leading cause of death for both men and women.

Cardiovascular health encompasses many different facets of our bodies: circulatory system, the heart structure itself, cholesterol, blood pressure, stroke, arrhythmias, and so much more! Our age and lifestyle all have a huge bearing on our heart health, as do genetics and environmental factors. In order to keep our spiritual heart fit, it's important that we keep the physical organ healthy and functioning.

The hardest working organ in the body is the heart. The essential components of the human cardiovascular system are the heart, blood, and blood vessels. The circulatory system circulates the blood around the body oxygenating the cells, delivering nutrients from the food you eat, and carrying away waste products. The digestive system works with the circulatory system to provide the nutrients the system needs to keep the heart pumping. We are, indeed, fearfully and wonderfully made!

An article published in 2010 in the "Iranian Journal of Nursing and Midwifery Research" found that the quality of sleep in heart disease patients was significantly improved after aromatherapy with lavender oil. Therefore, using aromatherapy can improve the quality of sleep and health. (4)

According to a 2012 study in the "European Journal of Preventive Cardiology," the essential oils which form the basis of aromatherapy for stress relief are also reported to have a beneficial effect on heart rate and blood pressure following short-term exposure -- and may therefore reduce the risk of cardiovascular disease. (5)

Our physical heart can be damaged by many things, including stress and fear. The Bible tells us in Proverbs 12:25 *Anxiety weighs down the heart, but a kind word cheers it up.* Anxiety is a byproduct of fear and the Lord encourages us to put our faith above our fears. John 14:27 reminds us, *Do not let your hearts be troubled and do not be afraid.*

INFUSED

For many of us, walking in faith is a daily practice. Many days, we hang on, minute to minute, as we often fall prey to fear and anxiety in our everyday lives. There are essential oils that can help steer us away from pressing anxiety and stress, thereby reducing the strain, both spiritual and physical, on our hearts.

Oils and oil infused products help our bodies absorb nutrition from the foods we eat. I will assume that's not Twinkies and chips!

Thyme, Frankincense, and Clove are essential oils that help to safeguard against the damaging effects of the environment, diet, and aging.

Ylang Ylang supports positive mood and energy. Simply inhaling this using a diffuser or applying to the abdomen has a direct correlation to sustaining heart health.

Lemongrass is a wonderful oil to support healthy cholesterol levels. I was told I was borderline on needing medicines to control mine. Simply adding this oil to my daily routine has brought me into healthy heart levels. Lemongrass supports the heart by strengthening vascular walls and dilating blood vessels. (6)

Lavender essential oil is very common for stress relief. A simple search of WebMD or other Government medical sites will provide a lot of research supporting its sedating effects. It may even relax certain muscles. It also seems to have antibacterial and antifungal effects.

Incense is mentioned 68 times in the Bible in which 54 of these instances the oils Frankincense, Myrrh, and Galbanum are referenced. Incense is translated from the Hebrew/Greek *frankincense* and is referring to the oil. It was valued more than gold in ancient times. Researchers have found the sesquiterpenes in Frankincense are able to go beyond the blood brain barrier and thus elevates the mind to overcome stress and despair.

Some of my favorite verses that include the Lord directly commanding the use of oils:

Exodus 30:34 *Then the LORD said to Moses, Take fragrant spices--gum resin, onycha and galbanum--and pure frankincense, all in equal amounts*

Leviticus 2:1-2 *And when any will offer a meat offering unto the Lord, his offering shall be of fine flour; and he shall pour oil upon it, and put frankincense thereon:*
2 And he shall bring it to Aaron's sons the priests: and he shall take thereout his handful of the flour thereof, and of the oil thereof, with all the frankincense thereof; and the priest shall burn the memorial of it upon the altar, to be an offering made by fire, of a sweet savour unto the Lord.

Best oils for the cardiovascular system: Lemon, Frankincense, Stress Away, Orange, Citrus Fresh, Lavender.

CHAPTER 2

DIGESTIVE SYSTEM: YOUR GUT REACTION

 **INSPIRED**

Have you ever had a gut feeling or intuition that led you to come to a conclusion about something and you can't logically explain how you arrived at that conclusion? Was it instinct? Have you ever had butterflies in the tummy? Our gut can tell us if something isn't quite right or even wrong. Part of the process is conscience. There is great evidence our gut is our second brain!

John 8:9 *Then those who heard it, being convicted by their conscience, went out one by one, beginning with the oldest even to the last. And Jesus was left alone, and the woman standing in the midst.*

Each of "those people that heard it" might not be able to give you a detailed explanation as to why their consciences convicted them, but they *felt* the wrongness deep within them. The gut.

In I Corinthians 10:25-33, Paul talks about conscience. Figure out what is wrong and until you know, don't violate your conscience. Feed on God's word so you can hear or even feel that 'still small voice' that even Elijah experienced.

Butterflies can be good.

Proverbs 23:16 *Yes, my inmost being will rejoice when your lips speak right things.*

Those butterflies can be from excitement and happiness, the kind where you can't eat because you're so happy.

We also have to admit our gut 'reaction' can be from foods we eat, stress, toxins, fear, and so much more! Our guts are amazing and so much flows in and out of them!

1 Corinthians 6:12-13 *Everything is permissible for me - but not everything is beneficial. But I will not be mastered by anything. Food is for the stomach and the stomach is for food, but God will do away with both of them.*

As a believer, I have the benefit of the Holy Spirit. I firmly believe I can achieve peace in my gut and shine a light from it too.

John 7:38 *He that believes in me, as the scripture have said, out of his belly shall flow rivers of living water.*
John 7:39 *By this he meant the Spirit, whom those who believed in him were later to receive. Up to that time the Spirit had not been given, since Jesus had not yet been glorified.*

Out of the bellies of Holy Spirit-filled believers flows rivers of living water because the Holy Ghost dwells there!

**God created it. Jesus paid for it.
And the Holy Spirit lives in it!
Take care of your body!**

 INFORMED

There was an article titled "How Smart is Your Stomach?" in the Ladies Home Journal (1966) in which it was reported that scientists believe there is a brain in your gut. Dr. J. D. Wood, Chairman of the Physiology Department at Ohio State University, calls the brain in your gut "the little brain", touting 100 million neurons which line the digestive tract from the esophagus to the colon. Scientifically termed the enteric nervous system, it has as many neurons or information centers as the spinal cord.

The following paragraph in the article reveals some very interesting observations:

> *The little brain is connected to the "big brain" by the vagus nerves, a bundle of nerve fibers running from the GI tract to the head. And, to the fascination of researchers, virtually all the classes of neurotransmitters found in the brain are also present in the gut. "The more we learn about the enteric nervous system, the more similar it seems to the brain," says Michael Gershon, M.D., chairman of anatomy and cell biology at*

*Columbia University College of Physicians and
Surgeons, in New York City.*

*Your gut is affected by toxins, foods, and even emotions
like fear and anxiety which can cause things such as
ulcers, skin disorders, nervous stomachs, heart attacks
and more. This should come as no surprise. Keep in
mind the little brain goes from the esophagus to the colon.*

1 Timothy 5:23 *No longer drink water exclusively, but use a
little wine for the sake of your stomach and your frequent
ailments.*

All health begins in your gut. What's incredible is that
researchers now believe up to 90% of all diseases can be
traced back in some way to the gut and health of the
microbiome. Memory loss, brain fog, and fuzzy thinking
can be frustrating and scary. Many people think those
symptoms are just a normal part of aging or the result
of bad genetics. However, the truth is backed by
science. Up to 90% of all Alzheimer's cases are caused
by diet, lifestyle, and environmental factors (NOT
genetics). And the #1 place you have the most control
over your level of risk is in what you eat!

Do you know what the human microbiome is? A vast
complex ecosystem of bacteria and microbes located
within our bodies that helps us to control weight, fight
infection, regulate sleep, and more. The vast majority of
the bacterial species that make up our microbiome live
in our digestive systems...our gut. What is colonized in
our gut can affect everything from our ability to regulate
emotions, our immune responses, and even our skin. As

studies continue to unearth the connection between the gut and the rest of the body, we are reminded more and more that we are not a series of small interdependent pieces functioning in a body. We are a whole vessel, complex and beautifully designed to function seamlessly. Taking care of our gut benefits our entire well-being and keeps our bodies true to their original, amazing design.

INFUSED

The environmental toxins in your home are killing off your microbiome day by day. The bacteria in your digestive system ensures the proper assimilation of the nutrients you need. Your microbiome is determined by the food you eat to the air you breathe and by every chemical cleaner you use and product you put on the body. Did you know that 70% of your immune system stems from your digestive system?

You can help to balance the health of your digestive system with diet and exercise, but there are a few other things to add for extra support.

Essential oils like Thyme, Oregano, and Lemongrass make an unfriendly environment for yeast and fungus. Use the oils 6-8 hours prior to using a good high potency probiotic.

Probiotics promote healthy digestion and normal intestinal function, and even better sleep and mood.

Oils for digestive health include: Fennel, Peppermint, Ginger, Lemon, Clove, Nutmeg, Oregano, Tarragon, Mountain Savory

CHAPTER 3

IMMUNE SYSTEM: YOUR DEFENSE SYSTEM

 **INSPIRED**

God created our bodies to be vigilant against what could harm us. The immune system is your body's own defense system that consists of a variety of structures and processes that protect us from pathogens, toxins, viruses, bacteria, and various other things with barriers. Think of it as a tiny army constantly protecting you on a microscopic level!

Exodus 23:25 *Worship the LORD your God, and his blessing will be on your food and water. I will take away sickness from among you…*

3 John 1:2 *Dear friend, I pray that you may enjoy good health and that all may go well with you, even as your soul is getting along well.*

Jeremiah 30:17 *But I will restore you to health and heal your wounds,' declares the LORD*

INFORMED

In Exodus 30:22-31, 34-36, God gives recipes for a Holy Anointing Oil and a Holy Incense with instructions on their uses. The anointing oil is to be used, not only to anoint and consecrate the Levite priests, but also to clean the altar of sacrifice. It was used to clean all of the instruments of the altar, including the laver, a bowl of water next to the altar for washing hands between sacrifices. This cleaning ritual was done daily.

If you think about it, a place where animals were sacrificed every day, sometimes hundreds in a day, could create an environment that would promote the growth of harmful bacteria, viruses, fungi, and parasites. These could, in turn, cause chronic sickness among the priests and personnel of the synagogues as well as epidemics among the people at large. But the Bible does not mention any instance of diseases caused by the environment of the altar and its surroundings.

It turns out that the ingredients of the Holy Anointing Oil (Oils of Cinnamon, Cassia, Calamus, and Myrrh) are all highly antimicrobial, meaning they are effective against bacteria, viruses, fungi, and parasites. Because the priests and their assistants actually used the anointing oil to clean and wipe all of the articles and surfaces on or around the altar on a daily basis, a pathogenic environment was never allowed to develop. Meanwhile, as the oil was applied during the daily cleaning process, the priests and assistants were breathing them into their bodies and were thus boosting their immune systems to resist any form of microbial attack.

Thus, you can see that the Holy Anointing Oil was for more than ceremonial purposes and a support for worship. (7)

Your immune system is your body's natural defense system that helps fight against dangerous invaders. It is very complex, consisting of many different systems, all working hard to protect your body from harmful microbes and illnesses.

Your skin, for example, is often the first line of defense against microbes. The skin cells produce and secrete antimicrobial proteins and immune cells.

Bone marrow produces all the different white blood cells, including the cells that develop into T cells.

Your thymus, a small organ located in the upper chest, is where T cells mature and go on to recognize and kill virus-infected cells.

The lymphatic system is a huge player in your immune response. This vast network serves as a conduit for travel and communication for immune cells between tissues and the bloodstream.

Your spleen, an organ located behind the stomach, has immune cells enriched into specific areas and can recognize and respond to blood-borne pathogens.

Another important defense system is your mucosal tissues. Think lungs, eyes, and reproductive tracts. These entry points are defended by secretions that contain enzymes that can destroy bacteria.

Our bodies were made to function perfectly, but things like diet, stress, exposure to toxins, and previous illnesses all act as small chinks in the armor of our immune systems. In order to keep this process running as smoothly as possible, we can help this amazing defense system by making sure it's well supported. More and more, scientists are finding that your gut and your immune system and your emotional well being all go hand in hand.

The Lord has provided good food, stress management, and help to defend against invaders.

INFUSED

I really do not need to stress the importance of diet and exercise here. You are hit with that on a daily basis from various angles. You picked up this book for more guidance on what OTHER natural ways there are to support the immune system.

So, I will assume you already know the importance of eating organic foods and removing toxins from your home. I will touch more on toxins in the skin section.

There are essential oils that are known as immunostimulants. These oils stimulate and build up the body's first line of defense against invaders. Oils such as Clove, Tea Tree and Thyme help with the production of white blood cells and there are at least 40 more!

Get lymphatic support with Basil, Lemon, Juniper, Lavender, and Helichrysum. Reduce mucus with Sage, Eucalyptus, Cypress, Cedarwood, Frankincense, and all varieties of Balsam.

How about general tonic oil? I could list a hundred here, but here are a few of my favorites...all of the citrus oils, Clove, Juniper, Cinnamon, Frankincense, Myrrh, Rose Vetiver, and Cistus.

CHAPTER 4

THE SKELETAL SYSTEM: THE SKELETON DANCE

 **INSPIRED**

Rom 12:21 *Offer your bodies as a living sacrifice - holy and pleasing to God-this is you true and proper worship.*

Proverbs 17:22 *A joyful heart is good medicine, but a broken spirit dries up the bones.*

Ecclesiastes 11:5 *Just as you do not know the path of the wind and how bones are formed in the womb of the pregnant woman, so you do not know the activity of God who makes all things.*

Muscle affects your behavior, mood, and motivation. Staying fit is a way to worship!

The problem with a living sacrifice is that it can crawl off the altar!

God did give us bones, ligaments, and muscles to be able to crawl, but when we do crawl, it shouldn't be for the fallen TV remote. Our motivation to stay fit is always to please God. We take care of our bodies so He can use us more effectively. Dedicate your body to His service!

Is this easy? No, it isn't. I give in to delicious custard and the occasional pizza, although I know I will pay the price for doing so. I know what is good for me and what is not. Many of us fall into the trap of believing that we are denying ourselves of guilty pleasures, but that's a lie. Many moons ago, we never would be eating how and what we do today. We have become dashboard diners. We have been slowly lead down this road to think Twinkies and chips count as nutrition. Consuming excess sodium in your diet and food devoid of vitamins and minerals can be harmful to your skeletal system, causing bone and mobility loss.

I wasn't getting diagnosed with early osteoporosis because I was fit and providing my body with the nutrition needed. Thankfully, I was motivated to reverse that early diagnosis.

 **INFORMED**

I loved the song I sang as a child called the Skeleton Dance. It went through the body singing "the hip bone's connected to the…"

There are 45 or more verses in the Bible on bones -- rottenness in bones, dry bones, rattling of bones, fat on bones, and even Eve was made with a rib bone from Adam.

Bones provide more than a framework for muscles, tissues, and skin. Our bones, all 206 of them, store very important minerals, nutrients, and lipids. Bones produce blood cells that nourish our bodies and play a critical role in protecting against infection. They protect vital organs like our heart, lungs, and brain. The spinal cord, which is the pathway for messages between the brain and the body, is protected by our spinal column. Bones build continually throughout life as the body renews the bone's living tissue.

Joints are where two or more bones connect and play a pivotal role (pun intended) in movement and stability. They connect bones within your body, bear weight, and enable you to move. Joints primarily consist of bones, muscles, synovial fluid, cartilage, and ligaments. Healthy joints aid us in movement, flexibility, and mobility and ensure that we are able to maintain a full range of motion.

Muscles make up approximately half of our body weight. They are designed to contract to produce motion. In addition to movement, muscle contraction also fulfills some other important functions in the body, such as posture, joint stability, and heat production as well as more subtle movements involving facial expressions, eye movements, and respiration. Muscles are responsible for allowing small movements such as chewing and digesting food to large movements involving strength like picking up something heavy. Even when you are sitting still or sleeping, your muscles move, keeping you breathing and your heart beating. The human body has more than 600 muscles!

A healthy diet, weight bearing exercise, and simply stretching can go a long way in keeping you moving!

# INFUSED

As we age, changes occur in our bones. Osteoporosis (porous bone) is when too much calcium has been dissolved and not replaced, leaving us with poor bone density that can easily fracture. Osteomalacia (soft bones) is when not enough calcium was deposited in childhood, leaving us with pain, muscle weakness, and rubbery bones.

Changes also occur in joint soft tissue causing swelling, pain, and loss of mobility for the opposing bones causing Osteoarthritis. A more serious form of the disease is Rheumatoid arthritis. The latter is actually an autoimmune disease, where the body is producing antibodies against joint tissue. Remember the immunity chapter?

The most common joint pain is arthritis. This is when inflammation causes pain, stiffness, and even fatigue. **The addition of essential oils can help along with regular management of sleep and diet. Peppermint, Lemongrass, Black Pepper, Marjoram, Wintergreen, and Vetiver are all great oils to use to support joints.** Using them in salves is a wonderful way to have relief all day.

Muscles become sore, tired, and tight from sport injuries, simple exercise, or even stress. Like me, you may just want to relax and get relief from aches and pains. **Basil is relaxing to smooth muscle and Marjoram helps to regenerate smooth muscle tissue. Spruce is another good choice to reduce pain and inflammation and Wintergreen is beneficial in relieving discomfort to bones, muscles, and joints.**

Essential oils can offer relief! Try Clove, Fennel, German Chamomile, Juniper, and Balsam Fir. Add to a hot bath with Dead Sea salts or Himalayan Salt.

CHAPTER 5

THE INTEGUMENTARY SYSTEM: YOUR COAT OF ARMOR

 INSPIRED

Eph 5:29 *For no one ever hated his own flesh, but nourishes and cherishes it, just as Christ does the church.*

Job 10:10-11 *Did You not pour me out like milk And curdle me like cheese; Clothe me with skin and flesh, And knit me together with bones and sinews?*

Ezekiel 37:6 *I will put sinews on you, make flesh grow back on you, cover you with skin and put breath in you that you may come alive; and you will know that I am the LORD.*

We pay a lot of attention to what we put in our mouths. We read food labels and see how much sugar, fat, and whole grains are in food products. So, why not pay just as much attention to what we put on our skin? That includes personal care as well as cleaners and laundry products!

Your skin health, like your overall health, comes down to stopping what you shouldn't be doing and starting something that you should! Stop putting harmful things on your body!

 **INFORMED**

The skin is an organ, your largest, and it has a big job and deserves special care. The skincare industry is huge, mainly because we all are either desiring the fountain of youth or tackling skin issues like eczema, psoriasis, and acne. Besides the obvious basics of diet, hydration, sleep, and balanced hormones for glowing skin, there are things you can add to that foundation.

Ditch the chemicals. The number of chemicals and toxins in our environment is increasing and our bodies are sponges to these toxins. It's not a matter of IF, but HOW, these toxins are affecting us. Acne, eczema, dry skin and oily skin are all indications that poor elimination of toxins is occurring in one of the primary routes of elimination. Endocrine-disrupting chemicals (EDCs) interfere with the production, transport, breakdown, binding, and elimination of hormones.

Chemicals are absorbed into the body through the skin. Putting chemicals on the skin may actually be worse than eating them. Toxins that enter through the skin can enter the bloodstream and cause harm before they are filtered by the liver. Because the skin is our body's largest organ, what we put on it and come in contact with gets absorbed into our bloodstream and integrated into our body tissues.

The skin is not a impermeable coat of armor on our body! Of course it protects our body, but it is highly permeable.

Our skin is also our body's thinnest organ. Only 1/10th of an inch separates our delicate organs from all sorts of toxins, many of which have estrogen-mimicking effects that can destroy all of our good health intentions.

With all the pollutants in the environment today, it is important that we use personal care and cleaning products that are made from natural and healthy ingredients.

Generally, in just one square inch of skin, you'll find all of these important functions going on:
      650 sweat glands
      100 sebaceous (oil-producing) glands
      78 heat sensors
      13 cold sensors
      165 structures that perceive pressure
      1,300 nerve endings
      19 yards of blood vessels

And every one of those roles can be influenced by what the skin comes into contact with.

INFUSED

This is where essential oils come into play. They bring the health-giving benefits of nature to your pores directly.

Melaleuca, aka Tea Tree Oil, and Oregano essential oils are considered antifungal and can be

used topically with a carrier oil to treat a variety of fungal skin conditions.

Oils like Frankincense to tone and promote new cells to grow, Rosemary to reduce and stop free radicals from breaking down the skin's elasticity, Myrrh for rejuvenating, Lavender and German Chamomile for soothing, Geranium for regenerating, Tea Tree for inflammation, Lemon for brightening, Lemongrass for excess oil production, and Carrot Seed to help stop the breakdown of healthy skin cells, just to name a few!

CHAPTER 6

THE NERVOUS SYSTEM: GETTING ON YOUR NERVES?

 **INSPIRED**

Some things are not necessarily wrong, they're just not necessary. Most choices you make in life are not really a matter between good and bad. They're more a matter of what's best for you. The Bible talks about this in 1 Corinthians 10:23: *I have the right to do anything,' you say— but not everything is beneficial. 'I have the right to do anything'— but not everything is constructive.*

Psalm 139:23-24 *Search me, God, and know my heart; test me and know my anxious thoughts. See if there is any offensive way in me, and lead me in the way everlasting.*

Psalm 121:1-2 *I lift up my eyes to the mountains— where does my help come from? My help comes from the Lord, the Maker of heaven and earth*

 **INFORMED**

Ever hear the expression, "You are getting on my nerves?"

Anything pertaining to nerves is going to be neurological, so it stands to reason that it encompasses the brain and the spinal cord (which comprise the central nervous system) and a network of nerves called the peripheral nervous system. The brain sends out messages to the body and the body reacts by triggering hormones. So, together with the endocrine system, the nervous system regulates and tries to maintain a state of homeostasis -- the normal state of the body.

The message gets there via the nerves. Every nerve goes through the spine (except the olfactory nerves through the sinuses). This is why damage to the back is so catastrophic. Electrical impulses travel through the spine and keep our body systems ticking through the peripheral nervous system. There are additional nervous systems within the peripheral system, but that's another book!

Think of nerves like a complicated telephone network consisting of lots of connections to send information from one part of the body to the next. This vast and complicated network relays sensory information from the surrounding world, helps send messages to your muscles, and helps keep your autonomic processes (like digestion and breathing) working efficiently.

 **INFUSED**

Nerves. This is where serious aromatherapy starts. Nervous tissue is comprised of three types of neurons: sensory, motor, and connector neurons. The brain alone contains an estimated 12 billion neurons!

These nerves affect everything...blood flow, bowel movements, growling stomachs, sweating, chills, ability to pick up objects, heart rate, breathing, and reflexes to name just a few.

Important nutrients are needed to support the nervous system such as proteins, amino acids, the B-complex vitamins and minerals.

For stress relief and relaxation for tense moments and feelings of anxiousness, try Lavender, Chamomile, Ylang Ylang, Rose, Cedarwood, Patchouli, and Vetiver.

For uplifting the spirit, any citrus essential oil is great - orange, lemon, tangerine. My personal favorite is orange. Jasmine is amazing for happiness, but it does come with a much higher price tag than your citrus oils.

CHAPTER 7

THE ENDOCRINE SYSTEM: THE HORMONE SHUFFLE

 **INSPIRED**

Genesis 5:2 *Male and female he created them, and he blessed them and named them Man when they were created.*

Prov 21:20 *There is precious treasure and oil in the dwelling of the wise.*

Galatians 5:22-23 *But the fruit of the Spirit is love, peace, longsuffering, gentleness, goodness, faith, meekness, temperance: against such there is no law.*

Some days we would love to nail down just one of the Fruits of the Spirit for a full 24 hours! There is not a woman or man on the planet that doesn't do an eye roll at the mention of hormones. Those wonderful little chemicals run around in the body, which seem to be in a constant state of imbalance. They are essential to life and their delicate balance can be easily upset causing all kinds of consequences. They rule. At one point in my life, my hormones were *way* out of control. I knew it. There were times I felt like I was sitting on a cloud, looking down, and thinking that I wouldn't want to know me either! Today there are oils in my home, and it's all good.

 **INFORMED**

The Endocrine System involves the organs of the body that produce hormones. This system aids our body in regulating metabolism, growth and development, and tissue function. It can also play a large role in moods. If you've ever felt like you're on a hormonal roller coaster, you certainly know that to be true!

As far back as 200 B.C., Chinese healers extracted sex and pituitary hormones from human urine for medicinal purposes using the sulfate mineral gypsum and the chemical compound saponin which was derived from the seeds of a flowering plant to learn about hormones. More recent study on the endocrine system didn't begin in earnest until the 19th Century, and we are still learning more and more each day. The most common endocrine disorder in the world is diabetes, affecting almost 100 million people in the United States alone.

Your endocrine system needs support. Life started in a garden, and we would do well getting back to one! Sunshine, fresh herbs and vegetables, fresh water, fresh air, lots of movement, and lots of rest.

My reality isn't exactly a garden. It consists more of artificial light, sitting at computers, too much light in bedrooms, and not getting enough sleep. Melatonin, your fountain of youth, is created in total darkness. It's hard to produce with all those blue lights from electronics.

Today's typical human also has to contend with polluted water filled with heavy metals, petro chemical substances, chemicals, and other hormone disruptors. Air pollution from such sources as cars and industry in urban areas and herbicides and pesticides in rural ones are also toxic. Our food supply has also been altered drastically and finding good quality foods is getting harder. Opt for organic and homegrown when at all possible. We eat way too much sugar! The liver needs some sour infusion for health. Many of us don't move enough. We know we need to, but most of us never make it through 2 months of a gym membership!

We are also subjected to a lot of external stressors, which complicates all of our bodily systems. We never seem to get to relax and restore, hence the plethora of yoga and meditation classes popping up all the time.

Exercising regularly, eating well, and avoiding toxins as much as possible are the obvious ways you can support your endocrine system to be at it's best. Alcohol can impair the regulation of blood-sugar levels by interfering with certain hormones, reduce testosterone levels in men, and increase the risk of osteoporosis by disrupting a calcium-regulating hormone called parathyroid hormone. Changing your lifestyle, one small step at a time, can make a huge difference in how well your body is able to function.

INFUSED

All the factors named above can affect the Endocrine system, but there are ways you can support your Endocrine system with essential oils!

For your sex glands, use Cypress on the bottom of your feet and move! Walk and bring those knees up high. Shower and shampoos also affect this system. Try Shutran for men and Dragon Time for women. Both of these are from Young Living.

Thyroid function can be impaired by too much stress, not enough sleep, and environmental toxins (cleaner, personal care, makeup). A healthy thyroid requires fresh, organic food. Try grass fed beef and wild caught fish.

Myrtle has been researched by Dr. Daniel Penoel for normalizing hormonal imbalances of the thyroid and ovaries as well as balancing the hypothyroid. (8)

If your liver is overloaded with toxins, switch out conventional grains for Einkorn and take a good probiotic. Use Juvaflex Essential Oil Blend by Young Living and/or Juva Power, also by Young Living, on the right side of your ribs and cover with a warm moist towel.

To help with sleep, diffuse Lavender with Cedarwood. Other tree oils work well because of high terpene levels.

To support the thymus gland, you can try Endoflex by Young Living on the chest. Help wake it up!

You can focus on staying hydrated by using some of the Vitality oils to add flavor to plain water.

To aid weight loss, Slique Tea, an Oolong tea with cinnamon bark that helps give it a light sweet taste, reduces cravings because of the Frankincense powder in it.

Orange colored glasses will help protect the endocrine system from the blue computer light and light from the television. Blue light inhibits melatonin production, imperative for restful sleep.

Your Pineal gland is responsible for over 800 processes that happen in the body. To help support this gland, Cedarwood essential oil can be used on fingertips to gently tap the top of the head, then put in hands and cup over nose and mouth and breathe in for a few minutes. Just relax.

Sandalwood cream rejuvenates the skin's lower layers. Helps you sleep too

CHAPTER 8

CBD: THE NEW KID ON THE BLOCK

This last chapter is dedicated to CBD oil. It is getting a lot more attention lately and people are starting to awaken to its many benefits.

However, CBD has a serious identity problem. It's like when you have an out-of-control sibling and people think you must be just like them. Same family, same concerns?

Let's start with terms. Cannabis, marijuana, and hemp do not describe the same thing. Cannabis is a genus of the flowering plant, which produces both marijuana and hemp. Yes, they come from the same plant species, but have completely different effects on the body.

If you want to get high? Use Marijuana. It has a high THC content.
If you don't want to get high? Use Hemp.

Hemp has been found in pottery shards over 10,000 years old and records of cultivation for fiber in China dates back to 2800BC. Marijuana medical usage dates back to 2000BC. A full history can be found in the book <u>The Power of CBD & Essential Oils</u> by Dr.

Oliver Wenker. This book has 63 pages of over 890 scientific references!

Marijuana is cultivated for its primary psychoactive phytocannabinoid, tetrahydrocannabinol, or THC, for recreational and medicinal value. Hemp has been cultivated for thousands of years for food, clothing, fiber, and fuel and is one of the world's oldest domesticated crops.

So, the so-called 'new kid' is really very old.

Let me simply state some facts:
*Hemp is easily grown, eco friendly, and grows fast.
* Hemp is hardy, meaning it needs less pest management and can be harvested up to 3 times per year.
*Hemp is known to pull toxins out of the earth. Farmers know it is regenerative to the soil. Within a few seasons, the soil will have the same composition as organic soil. It's like a liver for your garden!
*Hemp crops started in the Middle East because of their hardiness and versatility.
*Hemp makes rope, cloth, canvas, fiberglass, paper, and building material.

History of Hemp

1600s American settlers originally HAD to grow hemp. The founding fathers were actually punished if they weren't growing a certain amount of hemp. Early settlers in North America brought hemp seeds with them and began cultivating the crop in Jamestown in the early 1600s. Hemp fibers were used for clothing, building materials, sails, and weapons. In 1619, The Virginia Assembly established that all citizens were required to grow hemp. The Colonists used the hemp to produce cordage, cloth, canvas, sacks, and paper during the years leading up to the Revolutionary War.

1941 Henry Ford made a fully hemp car that ran on bio fuel. He made the car from fiberglass made from hemp that was actually stronger than steel. However, the steel industry was going strong. Hemp was a threat.

1920-1950 Several things happened to cause the crash of hemp production, but to keep this short, I will only give a brief overview. It may not surprise you to learn that it was all about money and not about public interest.

There was a media blitz to make hemp illegal by prominent politicians and businessmen. Two men were primarily responsible for the modern federal-level legal prohibition of marijuana. Harry Anslinger was an ambitious government bureaucrat who, in 1930, became Director of the Federal Bureau of Narcotics (the precursor to today's Drug Enforcement Agency). Anslinger was appointed thanks to nepotism by his wife's uncle, Treasury Secretary Andrew Mellon (of Mellon Bank, one of the most powerful financial institutions in the world at the time). William Randolph

Hearst was a publishing and timber mogul who owned major newspapers and popular magazines. Disturbed by hemp's "billion-dollar crop" success and its impact on their plastic market shares, American industrialists, led by William Randolph Hearst and DuPont executives, initiated a smear campaign to destroy the lucrative hemp market. Painting hemp as the "evil weed" because it shared the same genus and species as marijuana, their conniving strategy worked. Anslinger drew upon the social stereotypes and racial prejudices of the day to stigmatize cannabis.

Hearst and Anslinger were supported by Lammot du Pont of the DuPont chemical company and a variety of pharmaceutical corporations, all of which had a financial interest in defeating cannabis to promote their own products. Due to advancements in harvesting equipment, hemp was also a threatening competitor to wood. Using Anslinger's position within the U.S. government and leveraging Hearst's empire of newspapers and magazines as propaganda outlets, the two concocted outlandish stories, all of which depicted marijuana as being more destructive than it was. Their sensationalistic stories described pot as an evil drug that led to murder, rape, and insanity. Their plan worked, and they were able to change public opinion and perception about hemp and the industry. Hemp became a controlled substance in 1970 when Congress passed the Controlled Substance Act, lumping hemp in with marijuana.

2018 Farm bill passed to bring back the hemp industry by removing it and some cannabis products from the CSA. The hemp industry is about ready to explode.

Hemp versus Marijuana

Hemp:
Taller and denser
Both female and Male plants
Useful crop

Marijuana:
Short full plant
No male plants used. Male plants are pulled up.
Female only. They get frustrated not being pollinated by the male plant and produce more resin. That resin is the THC.

What is CBD & How Does It Work?

CBD stands for Cannabiniol, which is a phytocannabinoid discovered in 1940. There are 133 cannabinoids found in the hemp plant. CBD actually reverses the psychotropic effects of THC. CBD receptors are found all over the body. Researchers believe we have up to 15 different receptors in our bodies, but we currently know of two main types of CBD receptors in the body. CB1 is found mostly in the central nervous system, connective tissues, and glands, whereas CB2 is mostly found in the immune system and its structures like lymph nodes, spleen, thymus, and bone marrow.

These CB receptors comprise the Endocannabinoid System. The Endocannabinoid System, or ECS, regulates processes in the body that supports homeostasis, the balance of the body. It controls endocannabinoids, the messenger molecules your body produces, and the endocannabinoid receptors or doorways on every cell that accepts them, called CB1 and CB2. The ECS responds to many plants and essential oils.

CBD is adaptogenic just like essential oils, meaning they know where to work in the body and bring the body to a healthy level of balance.

How can CBD help us?

Immune system - decreases inflammation and immune reaction, like autoimmune disorders, as it decreases antibody production. We KNOW it decreases symptoms of asthma, Hashimoto's, flu, rheumatoid arthritis, Celiac disease, and allergies.

Brain support - neuro-protectant, decreases stress, decreases seizures, antipsychotic, antidepressant, reduces pain, increases sleep, and improves mood. There is known support and improvement for every recognized brain disorder out there such as addiction, Alzheimers, Parkinsons, and schizophrenia. A lot of new and exciting research is currently underway!

Gut - reduces inflammation, reduces nausea and vomiting, decreases cramping and spasms. CBD helps regulate the appetite. THC increases the appetite. Again, its adaptogenic.

Eyes - supports healthy eyes. Decreases glaucoma and its symptoms by regulating eye pressure.

Bone - increases bone density.

Cardiovascular - heart protectant, increases blood flow and circulation, prevents plaque formation, supports healthy lipid levels and lowers blood pressure.

Other - muscle relaxant, antibacterial, vertigo, supports healthy sugar levels, cell growth and skin.

There are no known dangers or addiction issues from using CBD.

A Word of WARNING!

It's important to know where the plant was grown and what distilling practices were used and how a company extracts the CBD. As I noted above, hemp is known to pull toxins out of the Earth and is regenerative to the soil. If the plant is removing toxins from the soil, it is now contained in its biomass. There seems to be a public safety threat, due to the fact there are no EPA regulations of approved chemicals used on the crops. Toxic chemicals are being found in both marijuana and hemp crops. Heavy metals are being intentionally added to increase market weight. Knowing the distillation practices and how a company extracts the CBD is important too. Solvents and pesticides may be left over in the products.

Look for Seed to Seal certification of hemp and essential oils!

Full spectrum VS Isolate

CBD is often labeled as full spectrum or CBD Isolate. Full spectrum has the possibility of THC. CBD Isolate contains nothing except pure, isolated CBD, there are no other cannabinoids, terpenes, or flavonoids. Unlike isolates, full-spectrum CBD products contain a full range of cannabinoids. However, with the addition of essential oils, we get the full spectrum benefits of CBD without the THC. The essential oils increase the effectiveness of the CBD.

The body recognizes natural...CBD aids in bringing it back to homeostasis...and that's a good thing!

FINAL THOUGHTS

The River of Life

Revelations 22
1 Then the angel showed me a river of the water of life, as clear as crystal, flowing from the throne of God and of the Lamb
2 down the middle of the main street of the city. On either side of the river stood a tree of life, bearing twelve kinds of fruit and yielding a fresh crop for each month. And the leaves of the tree are for the healing of the nations.
3 No longer will there be any curse. The throne of God and of the Lamb will be in the city, and his servants will serve him

Water restores, refreshes, and supports life. The trees of life are fed by the pure waters of the river that comes from the throne of God. The presence of God in Heaven is the health and happiness of the saints. The Greek word translated "healing" in this verse (*therapeia*) is the source of our English word "therapy." The fruit of the tree will surely contain many nutrients for happy, vigorous service by Christ's servants in the ages to come and so its leaves will contain a complex mix of compounds and constituents, substances useful for the health of God's people. Symbolically, then, these would be curative, life-sustaining provisions for our everlasting life. The source of the provisions is the royal throne of God and of the Lamb Jesus Christ.

The river of life and the tree of life are both symbols of the eternal life that the residents of Paradise will enjoy.

Psalm 139:16 *Your eye formed me...*God ordained days for us. He has a vision for your life. You can't fulfill it if you are not honoring your body!

What's Next?

Ephesians 2:10 *It is God himself who has made us what we are and given us new lives from Christ Jesus; and long ages ago he planned that we should spend these lives in helping others.*

I want you to share my passion of walking in God's power of healing. I want to train you in how to use essential oils. I want you to understand the power of God's medicine.
Without knowledge, people perish!

I want you to understand how to use essential oils along with diet to live abundantly. I want you to understand how using man made products are destroying your body. I want you to live in the power and freedom and the wisdom to choose life!

The Bible has a ton of scriptures about wisdom. Matthew 7:7 says, *Ask and it will be given to you, seek and you will find; knock and it will be opened to you. For everyone who asks receives and he who seeks finds, and to him who knocks it will be opened.*

I would love to offer you a 'Now What', a simple 4 month plan of action. It's a therapeutic model of aromatherapy and whole based nutritional supplements which can strengthen and balance the body. You will simply be educated on the different body systems and you choose how to support and maintain them with gentle guidance. It can be anything from weight to immunity to pain and even emotional support. It's personal to you and done in a one-on-one consultation with ongoing weekly support.

I would like to also offer you community. Rom 12 4:5 reminds us that *we are many parts of one body.* You will not make all the changes you need to make, plan to make, or even dream to make on your own. God wired us to need each other to encourage, love, and share with and support. You need the power of people around you and they need you too!

In order to learn more, please contact me at lifesparkaromatherapy@gmail.com to get started on your journey to health!

Follow us at:
www.facebook.com/LindaOviattLivingNaturally/
https://www.instagram.com/lindaoviatt/
http://lindaoviatt.ylsocial.net/

Seek the advice, wisdom, and knowledge of God. He freely gives. Then simply believe and step into the journey. Wisdom is knowledge applied!

Keep your body strong so you can serve others!
Honor it so you can accomplish God's mission for you!
Open your eyes to the provision he gave us in the garden
So you can take care of your body for service!

DISCLAIMER

The information provided in this book is simply designed to provide helpful information and suggestions on supporting healthy body systems. The contents of the book have not been evaluated by the FDA. The book is not meant to be used as or used for the diagnosis or treatment of any medical condition. The publisher and/or the author are not responsible for any damages or negative consequences from any treatment, action, application or preparation, to any person reading or following any information in this book. This book has been written for educational purposes only and to share my own personal story.

References are provided for informational use only.

Responsibility and consequences lie not with Lifespark Aromatherapy, LLC or Linda Oviatt. All advice, suggestions and references are taken at your own risk.

REFERENCES

1. Some of this information is found in the book, "Healing Oils of the Bible," but the antimicrobial benefits of the anointing oil and incense are more thoroughly discussed in the book and set of DVDs entitled "Healing: God's Forgotten Gift."

2. Aromatherapy, The Essential Beginning, D. Gary Young N.D.

3.https://www.cms.gov/research-statistics-data-and-systems/statistics-trends-and-reports/nationalhealthexpenddata/nationalhealthaccountshistorical.html

4. https://www.ncbi.nlm.nih.gov/pmc/articles/PMC3203283/

5. https://www.sciencedaily.com/releases/2012/11/121129093419.htm

6. Essential Oils Integrative Medical Guide, D. Gary Young N.D.

7. Healing Oils of the Bible, Dr. David Stewart

8. Essential Oils Desk Reference 6th Edition

LINDA'S SUGGESTED READING LIST

Essentials, Lindsey Elmore, PHARMD, BCPS

The Chemistry of Essential Oils Made Simple, Dr. David Stewart

The Power of CBD and Essential Oils, Dr. Oliver Wenker

Nutrition 101: Choose Life, Debra Raybern, Sera Johnson, Laura Hopkins

Supplements Desk Reference, Jen O'Sullivan

WHAT LINDA'S FOLLOWERS ARE SAYING

This book is a good road map for getting started on your journey of using essential oils. It is an informative overview of the historical, scientific, and spiritual aspects of oils and provides references for further study. Whether you are just beginning to explore the use of oils or have started using them and are wondering, "What's next?" you will find this book helpful.

-- Sally Berger, Educator and Program Coordinator

Linda Oviatt is your friend. She cares about your health. You'll feel that as you read her book, "Inspired, Informed, Infused" Her down to earth, straight to the point nature makes you want to learn more about oils and how they relate to your health and your worship. Her humor and easy to understand explanations make this an entertaining, educational, and enlightening experience.

-- Carrie Hyman, Executive Director, Main Street Mount Vernon

WHAT LINDA'S FOLLOWERS ARE SAYING

Linda's Oviatt's candidness is so relatable. As I started to read the book I got sucked in. I wanted to run out and get some oils and start thriving too. And that is exactly what happened. Such a breath of fresh air.

— Jennifer Watson, Owner, Affordable Farm Wow

Linda graciously shares her knowledge and insight so beautifully and with such a humble heart! Her unique flair for words combined with her passionate spirituality lays out a beautiful path for the reader to follow on their own journey to health. I'm so excited that she's sharing her message with the world!

— Lora Denton, Clarity Director at Masters In Clarity

Linda's unique brilliance is her ability to passionately explain what she's learned while inspiring others to rise to their best selves. She is a wealth of information, informing her audience on how to live in wellness, purpose and abundance. Linda Oviatt is one of the most genuinely caring people I've ever met and I'm honored to witness her journey, as she helps people embrace their health.

— Dolores Hirschmann, CEO at Masters In Clarity

ABOUT THE AUTHOR

I went from a successful and award winning sales career spanning 30 years to become the Founder and Executive Director of an award winning ministry serving the homeless children of Cobb county for over 10 years. I received the West Cobb Citizen of the Year award through the Cobb Chamber of Commerce in 2010 and the Jack C Vaughan Human Services award in 2014 for my work within the homeless community.

I retired from ministry in 2015, and I am now pursuing my passion for health and wellness after a turn in my own health led me to the benefits of essential oils and natural living. I became a Certified Aromatherapist in 2016, after realizing that my health had to take priority in my life. I am now a sought after Aromatherapist and speaker, informing and inspiring my audience on living above the wellness line using essential oils and natural living.

I am a closet artist, amateur gardener, live in blue jeans and a t-shirt whenever possible and if you leave the door open long enough, I could be headed for a cruise somewhere!

Today I combine an award-winning sales career, love of people and a passion for living naturally to make a change in this world, one drop at a time.